# "Faith it All"

T0159136

# *Faith*

# "Faith it All"

A spiritual guide when you are facing the storms of life.

## Joyce Ann Whitlock

authorHOUSE®

AuthorHouse™
1663 Liberty Drive
Bloomington, IN 47403
www.authorhouse.com
Phone: 1-800-839-8640

First published by AuthorHouse    5/2/2011

ISBN: 978-1-4634-0387-4 (sc)
ISBN: 978-1-4634-0386-7 (dj)
ISBN: 978-1-4634-0587-8 (ebk)

Library of Congress Control Number: 2011908222

Printed in the United States of America

Any people depicted in stock imagery provided by Thinkstock are models, and such images are being used for illustrative purposes only.
Certain stock imagery © Thinkstock.

This book is printed on acid-free paper.

# Contents

# Faith

# Dedication

To my beloved brother-in-law, Walter L. Hopkins, whose spirit lives through his lovely wife Barbara, his children and grandchildren: La Jauii, Leekel, Jeff, La Shanne, Roderick, Jontae, Jonathan Justin, Dorian, Jamal, Chance, Chace, Alicia, Ashley, Justin, Landon Walter, and Leland.

May he rest in peace.

# Faith

# Introduction

This is not a lengthy book full of words and chapters to sort through, but a reference guide to help individuals walk in faith as they take this journey of faith during the storms of life. No one is immune from storms. Storms are necessary for each of us because it is during those times; we have an opportunity to exercise our faith. Storms are necessary to equip us to help others and for the manifestation of our Lord and Savior. Finally, storms make us stronger because when we are in the midst of the storm, we are tossed on every side and become bruised but never broken much like a diamond.

The word diamond comes from the Greek word 'Adamas" which means indestructible; however, before one diamond is formed, Mother Nature has to toil the earth for millions of years. So, this faith journey is a process that will take its form overtime much like the formation of a diamond. As we continue to walk in faith, we will be able to withstand any storm regardless of its magnitude.

# Faith

# What is Faith?

**Hebrew 11: 1** defines faith as: *'The substance of things hoped for, the evidence of things not seen."*

Faith is mentioned in the New King James Version a total of 338 times. Fifty-eight (58) times in the Old Testament, and 280 times in the New Testament. Why is faith mentioned so many times in the bible? Faith is the foundation of Christianity.

Some examples where <u>faith</u> may be found are as follows in The New King James Version of the New Testament:

**Matthews 17: 20** *"Because of your unbelief; for assuredly, I say to you, if you have <u>faith</u> as a mustard seed, you will say to this mountain, Move from here to there, and it will move and nothing will be impossible for you.'*

**Matthews 25: 23.** *His Lord said to him, well done, good and <u>faithful</u> servant; you have been <u>faithful</u> over a few things, I will make you ruler over many things.*

There was an incident found in Matthews where a multitude had gathered before the Lord and disciples. One man reported to Jesus he had brought his epileptic son to the disciples but explained that they could not heal him. Jesus answered: *"Oh faithless and perverse generation, how long shall I be with you? How long shall I bear with you? Bring him to me."*

**2 Corinthians 5: 7** Paul tells us: *"We walk by faith, not by sight.'*

**Roman 10:17** *"So then faith comes by hearing, and hearing by the word of God."*

**Galatians 5:5** *"For we through the Spirit eagerly wait for the hope of righteousness by faith."*

**Ephesians 2: 8** *for by grace you have been saved through faith, and that not of yourselves."*

**2 Thessalonians 3:2** *"And that we may be delivered from unreasonable and wicked men: for all have faith."*

**Hebrew 11:6** *reminds* us the necessity of having faith: *But without faith it is impossible to please Him.*

**James 5:15** *"And the prayer of faith will save the sick and the Lord will raise him up. "And if he committed sins, he will be forgiven."*

Faith is mentioned Luke Chapter 19 verses 17 when Jesus gave a parable after he walked through Jericho. The large crowd who had followed Him thought the kingdom of God would appear immediately. Jesus began to describe to them how an official had gone on a far country to receive a kingdom and later returned. He later called ten of his servants and gave to them ten minas and asked them to conduct business for him until he returned.

He went on to explain how the citizens hated him and sent a delegation after him to protest his reigning over them. After receiving the kingdom, he returned; he commanded his servants to whom he had given minas to give their report to tell how much they earned by trading.

One servant reported; "Master, your minas has earned ten minas." He said, "well done, good servant because you were **faithful** in a very little, you will have authority over ten cities."

## <u>NOTES:</u>

# NOTES:

# Faith

# How Do You Weather the Storm?

1. First acknowledge the storm.

2. Second, recognize your emotions such as, hurt, anger, disappointment, sadness, fear, helpless, indecisiveness, and uncertainties of the future, etc.

3. Pray continually to the Creator confessing the above emotion(s) and confess that you are powerless. Remember the bible tells us to pray without ceasing and especially when storms arise.

4. Keep a daily journal of your prayers such as the date and what you prayed for that day.

5. Include fasting in your daily prayer life (this may be impossible if you have a health condition that prohibits you from fasting). Fasting can be first day of the week, or one hour per day. Advance to eight hours until twenty-four hours.

6. Read a bible scripture daily and maintain the date of each scripture you read. It is always helpful to start reading Psalms; it has been referred to as the blueprint that teaches us how to live especially when we are going through the storm.

# NOTES:

# Faith

# Why is Faith Necessary?

Jesus died on the cross and was resurrected. As believers, once we accept the Lord as our personal Savior and believe He died and was raised from the dead; we begin that very moment to walk in newness of faith. For that very reason; faith of the believer is essential because the resurrection was the greatest miraculous event in history and the basic principle of Christianity. As new believers, we no longer need miracles or supernatural things as Jesus performed while He was here on earth, nor do we have to bring a sacrificial offering because the Lord gave us the ultimate sacrificial gift for our sins, His life.

---

Jesus performed countless miracles before He was crucified. These miracles are recorded in the New Testament. First, let us review some of them.

**John 2: 7.** This was the first miracle Jesus performed. It was during a wedding where both Jesus and the disciples were invited. They ran out of wine. Jesus asked:" *Fill the water pots with water . . . draw some out now, and take it to the master of the feast."*

**Luke 7:12** describes how a widowed woman only son died and when Jesus came near the gate of the city, he witnessed a large crowd had gathered at the funeral. When the Lord saw the widowed woman, he had compassion for her and said:" Do not weep." Then He touched the coffin, and those who carried the body stood still. Jesus spoke: 'Young man, I say to you, arises." The dead son sat up and began to speak, and the Lord presented him to his mother.

Who could forget the story when Jesus raised Lazarus from the dead?

**John 11: 1-44** tells us Lazarus had been dead for four days and was buried. Jesus asked; "show me where he lay." Jesus called out in a loud voice: "Lazarus come out." Lazarus came forth with his feet and hands bound with grave clothes and his face muffled with a handkerchief. Jesus exclaimed: "Now unbind him, and let him go home."

There was another miracle during the time Peter's mother-in-law was ill with a fever found in Matthew **8:14-17**. Jesus healed her. Upon entering the house, he found her in bed. He simply touched her hand and the fever left. She got up and began to serve them!

**Matthews 8:1-4** we find a large crowd beginning to follow Jesus. During his walk, He found a leper who knelt in front of him. The leper said: "Sir if you want to, you can make me clean." Jesus stretched out His hand and placed it on the leper and asked him if he wanted to be cleaned. The leper replied, "of course I want to be clean." And at once, he was cleared of leprosy.

**John 4:43-54:** An official who had a dying son came to Jesus while he was in Galilee. Jesus went off to see him after the official begged him to come down and heal his son, who was by this time at the point of death. Jesus said to him: "I suppose you will never believe unless you see signs and wonders." The official said: "please come down before my boy dies." Jesus told him: "You can go home . . . your son is alive and well." The man then believed what Jesus said to him and went on his way. On the way back, his servants met him with the report; "your son lives." The official still lack faith because he asked the servant the hour when he got better. The servant told him it was the seventh hour the fever left his son. Then the father knew that it was the same hour in which Jesus said to him, "your son is alive and well." It was only then this father and whole household first believed.

Jesus, while on earth, performed miracles as His disciples and others watched Him. Yet, even after witnessing these miracles, the crowd and His disciples were faithless. This is evident when Jesus triumphantly entered the City of Jerusalem prior to the crucifixion. This same crowd witnessed Him demanded Lazarus to rise from the grave after being buried for four days **(John 12: 12-19)**. He entered Jerusalem riding a donkey. The crowd cried out! Hosanna Hosanna! Later that same crowd shouted Crucify Him! Crucify Him!

**Luke Chapter 23** gives us an account of the trial and crucifixion of our Lord and Savior. A multitude arose and led Him to Pontius Pilate. He was accused of perverting the nation, and refusing to pay taxes, saying He Himself was Christ, a King. Pilate wanted to release Jesus because he found Him guiltless. Yet when he gave the people the choice to choose between Jesus and a murderer, the crowd chose to release the murderer. They were insistent and demanded Jesus be crucified.

Jesus was crucified on Mt. Cavalry. According to St. Luke 23, it was the sixth hour after He was on the cross; darkness came over the earth until the ninth hour. Then the sun was darkened and the veil of the temple was torn in two. Jesus then cried out, 'Father into Your hands I commit my spirit." Then He took His last breath. It was only then the centurion saw what had happened that he glorified the lord saying, "Certainly this was a righteous Man."

Joseph, a councilman, went to Pilate and asked for the body of Jesus. He took the body down from the cross and laid it in a tomb where no one else had lain. There were women who followed Jesus from Galilee who observed the tomb and the manner in which the body was laid. They later returned and prepared spices and fragrant oils.

Yet on the first day of the week, the women came to the tomb bringing spices which they prepared, but found the stone had been rolled away from the tomb. After entering the tomb, they did not find the body of Jesus Christ. Two men suddenly appeared by them in shining garments. The two men asked; "Why do you seek the living among the dead? He is not here, but is raised! They were reminded how He had spoken to them saying; "The Son of Man must be delivered unto the hands of sinful men, and be crucified, and the third day rise again."

Then the women remembered and returned and shared all those things to the eleven disciples; however, the disciples did not believe them. One of the disciples, Peter, went to the tomb. Once he arrived, he saw the linen cloths and an empty tomb.

Luke goes on to tell how Jesus walked with two of the disciples the same day the tomb was found empty. As they were headed to a village called Emmaus, Jesus began to converse with them, but they did not recognize Him. When they returned to Jerusalem, the eleven disciples gathered and exclaimed; 'The Lord is risen indeed, and has appeared to Simon." They began to talk about things that had happened on the road, and as they spoke, Jesus appeared in the midst and said, "Peace to you." They were frightened; they thought they had seen a spirit. Jesus asked them: "Why do your doubts rise in your hearts?" 'My hands and my feet, that is I myself." "Handle me and see, for a spirit does not have flesh and bones as you see I have."

The disciples still did not believe. Jesus asked them for something to eat, and He ate in their presence. He explained the words He had spoken to them when He was still with them that all things must be fulfilled that were written in the Law of Moses and the prophets and the Psalms. He opened their understanding so they could understand the scripture. He commissioned them to stay in Jerusalem until they received the power from on high. He promised them that He would send the Promise of His Father upon them. Later He led them to the town of Bethany and then lifted His hands and blessed them and He departed into heaven.

Now we see how Luke explains how the disciples walked with the Lord prior to the crucifixion; yet they doubted. It was only when the Lord appeared to them twice and went on teaching them they began to understand and to believe. Also, the Lord promised that He would go to His father on their behalf and send them the Promise of

His father in order that they maybe equip to continue to teach the will of His Father in Jerusalem. We, too, if we believe Christ died on the cross for our sins and were raise from the dead on the third day, may have the same power given to the disciples. This power sustains us in time of trouble when we face the storms of life, but we must have faith. It is because of faith; we can go through any storm with confidence.

## NOTES:

# Faith

# When will Our Faith be Tested?

As stated earlier, no one is immune from storms. It is during these stormy seasons that our faith will be tested. Some examples of storms we may experience are:

- Death of a loved one
- Receiving a pink slip from your employer
- Diagnosed with cancer
- Family member diagnosed with Alzheimer's disease
- Adultery / Divorced
- Foreclosure Notice/Eviction Notice
- Family Feud
- Teenage daughter becomes pregnant
- Child gets arrested
- Friend/ Family betrayal
- Break-up/relationships
- Deciding to relocate/ resign from your job
- Having to suddenly live alone

- Funds are depleted with no source of income
- Forced to take early retirement

Now let's explore some of these storms and determine how our faith may be put into action.

## NOTES:

# Faith

# Death of a loved One

No one escapes death; we all must die just as our Savior did. But as believers, we should rejoice knowing we and our loved-one will live again just as the Lord was resurrected. If an individual has not accepted the Lord as his/her personal Savior, but confesses his or her sins, accepts the Lord as his/her personal Savior, and believes Jesus died on the cross before succumbing **(Roman 10:9),** the individual becomes a born again Christian and a member of the Royal Family instantaneously! We are saddened when a love one succumbs, but we can be assured if they died as a believer because their physical death is temporary.

I spoke with a chaplain at a local hospital concerning death. He explained during his lifetime how he witnessed death of countless individuals, believers and none believers. He said something so profound that has remained with me. He explained, once an individual dies, he/she recognizes the Creator. He went on to explain even none believers acknowledge the Creator prior to taking their last breath. This should be comforting knowing that a loved one is with the Creator and will live again, and more importantly, we will see them again.

**I Thessalonians 4: 13-18** explains it this way:

*But I would not have you to be ignorant, brethren, concerning them which are asleep, that ye sorrow not, even as others which have no hope. For if we believe that Jesus died and rose again, even so them also which sleeps in Jesus will God bring with Him. For this we say unto you by the word of the Lord, that we which are alive and remain unto the coming of the Lord shall not prevent them which are asleep. For the Lord Himself shall descend from heaven with a shout, with the voice of the archangel, and with the trump of God: and the dead in Christ shall rise first: Then we which are alive and remain shall be caught up together with them in the clouds, to meet the Lord in the air: and so shall we ever be with the Lord.*

Keep this bible passage close at-hand especially those days when your grieving seems overbearing on those cloudy days, or during major holidays, or when you stumble across an old picture or clothing item of the deceased. Secondly, on those days, begin to rejoice and praise the Lord for this temporary death. Praise him because there was no prolong suffering especially when the medical report projected otherwise. I am sure there is something to praise and rejoice about, and by doing so, this will assist you to go through the grief process with ease.

# NOTES:

# Faith

# Loneliness

Loneliness is a state of mind as a result of an individual electing to remain preoccupied with self-centeredness due to continual reflection of the past, or a loss of something or someone cherished. If an individual continues to remain preoccupied and self- centered, he/she could eventually drift into depression or could become ill with psychosomatic conditions such as, hypertension, ulcer, anxiety attack, and many other stress- related disorders.

A person may attempt to overcome loneliness by a myriad of ways such as, going on spending sprees, joining professional and religious organizations, or taking dance lessons etc. Joining various organizations may be therapeutic, but only temporarily. If the organization objective fails to provide a service, the individual will revert to loneliness because the organization failed to focus on the needs of others. Some individuals go on shopping sprees hoping to fill the void of loneliness. The end result may be more devastating having spent money he/she could not afford. Subsequently, the person encounters hardship both financially and emotionally, and not to mention the feeling of even a greater sense of loneliness because material possessions cannot solve loneliness.

Finally, during this state of preoccupation and self centeredness, an individual may seek an intimate relationship with another individual that may result in marriage. Unfortunately, the marriage will most likely dissolve because the individual expected the other person to fill the void of his/her loneliness. This is a mistake substantial number of individuals make when deciding to marry. No one can resolve the internal conflict of loneliness.

What causes Loneliness? The root cause of loneliness is the failure to redirect our emotions from self-centeredness to external concerns of our fellowman. Instead of seeking ways and opportunities to assist the needs of others, we choose to concentrate on ourselves. Helping others is a basic biblical principle each of us is charged as we travel along this journey called life. Remember Jesus said: "While I was hungry you fed me, when I was naked you clothed me, and while I was in prison, you visited me." The followers asked: "Lord when did we do these things?" He explained: "In as much as you done it unto the least of these, you done it unto me." (Matthew 25: 40).

So if you are constantly feeling lonely, begin to seek the needs of others, and by helping others, you will begin to full fill that internal emotional discord of loneliness.

## NOTES:

# *Faith*

# Receiving a Pink Slip

Years ago, when individuals were hired on a job, they expected to be employed for thirty years then retire. However, today an individual's average stay is five years or less. Employees' job may be subject to being outsourced, or the employer may cease operating as a result of filing bankruptcy. Regardless of the various reasons, receiving a pink-slip is painful, frightening, feeling abandoned, low self-esteem, and most challenging. Faith is required during this time considering the rate of unemployment that continues to soar. Remember **Hebrew Chapter 13 verse 5**: *Let your conversation be without covetousness; and be content with such things as ye have for He hath said, but remember the Lord promises to never leave us and to cast your fears on Him.*

How does an individual maintain his faith after receiving a pink slip when there is a mortgage payment and countless other monthly expenses? This is definitely a time when an individual's faith is being put to the test. Remember this is only a test. Meditate on the above scripture day and night. **Mark 16:16 reminds** us: "Faith without work is dead." So you must exercise your faith through action.

What should you do after receiving a pink slip?

First pray to the Creator and acknowledge your fears, insecurities, feeling of abandonment, anger, embarrassment, and helplessness, and any other emotions you may be experiencing. Pray daily and maintain a journal of your daily prays. It is especially important to record your emotions daily.

Apply immediately for unemployment.

Refer to the scripture **Hebrew 13:5** "I will never leave you nor forsake you." This is extremely helpful on those days when you are feeling abandoned. Compose your resume, or if you already have a resume, upgrade it to reflect your current job and skill-sets.

Inform your church family you have been laid off because there may be church members who may be aware of openings where they are employed, or they may own their company, and may have a need for your skills. Finally, ask the congregation to pray for you during this time; it is amazing how prayers work. Remember the bible tells us:

**Matthews 18: 20:** *"For where two or three are gathered together in my name, I am there in the midst of them."*

Search the web and register with professional organizations such as Career Builders. It is important to attach a resume on the web because there may be professional recruiters who are seeking individuals who possess your skills.

Remember to pray prior to seeking any new job. Ask the Lord to give you favor and remind Him of His word by saying, "Lord you promise to never to leave us, and you will be with us until the end of the age." Those days when you feel discouraged read **23rd Psalms** in its entirety. Never give up.

1991, was an economic downturn this country experienced when unemployment rate spiral upwardly. I was attempting to sell a condominium in Southern California. The unemployment rate in the State of California was 9.4% in 1999, and the national average was 7.4%. No one could ever imagine anyone could purchase a condominium in California with a decline of nearly 10% of its workforce. I kept the faith, and I turned my life over to Jesus. Shortly afterwards, I received an offer from a buyer during one of the toughest economical times this country experienced. To help clarify how miraculous my selling this condominium was, it is necessary to take you back in the 1990's which was during the **Savings and Loan crisis** (commonly referred to as the **S &L crisis**). This was the failure of 747 savings and loan associations. Yet this young buyer qualified for a loan to purchase my condominium. This was nothing more than a blessing as a result of my turning my life over to Jesus and keeping the faith in spite of the storm, of foreclosure.

## <u>NOTES:</u>

## NOTES:

# Faith

# Diagnosed with Cancer

Given a cancer diagnosis: Cancer may be defined when cells display an abnormal uncontrollable growth rate and begin to divide and invade adjacent tissue in the body. Receiving a diagnosis of cancer can feel as if a death penalty has been imposed. I witnessed two of my family members succumb from cancer. Sometimes individuals who have been diagnosed may live a long life and other live only weeks after the diagnosis is made. Life span depends on the type of cancer and the stage of the cancer.

We were not born to live forever on this earth. Because the bible tells us in **Hebrews 9: 27** "It is appointed for men to die once."

What do we do after being diagnosed with cancer?

Pray to the Creator to let His will be done. Asked Him to direct you in choosing the appropriate treatment options, and ask Him to orchestrate all treatments. Second, ask Him to speak to you when He determines to end treatment.

I have witnessed many individuals who were diagnosed with cancer throughout the years of my profession as a registered nurse. Having observed these individuals, I am thoroughly convinced when cancer invades the human body, it begins to prepare the body to return back to whence it was created. **Genesis 2: 7** tells us: "And the Lord God formed man of the dust of the ground, and breathed into his nostrils the breath of life, and man became a living being."

We were created from the soil and were created without food or water. Once an individual cancer advances, the individual begins to revert to the beginning of creation. This is evident because the individual begins to lose his/her appetite, and once we attempt to provide nutrition by artificial means the body will deteriorate more rapidly due to complications that result in the person developing fluid overload or aspiration pneumonia when we try to administer fluids intravenously or to feed through mechanical means. During this stage, we have to make the decision to withhold treatment, but to ensure palliative measures are done. This decision can be difficult to make because our natural instinct is to feed the person when he/she is unable to eat or drink, but the body is simply going back to its natural state.

We pray for our loved one and friends when they become gravely ill. Being present with them is most important. Also, let them know that it is ok for them to transition to their new spiritual home. I recall during my mother's last hour, my brother told her it was ok for her to leave. He assured her he would take care of me and it was then she seemed to become more restful and expired shortly thereafter. Death is not the end. Remember the bible tells us in **II Corinthians 5: 8** "We are confident, yes, well pleased rather to be absent from the body and to be present with the Lord."

## NOTES:

# Faith

# Family Member Diagnosed with Alzheimer

Alzheimer disease is a debilitating disease and unfortunately there is no cure. Symptoms may be overlooked when an individual simply begin to forget things as where he/she placed the car keys, forgetting important dates such as, doctor's appointments, household payments etc. The diagnosis is made after a series of cognitive behavioral examinations.

What do you do when a family member has been diagnosed? First, have a family meeting making them aware of the physician's diagnosis. It is important to involve family members because a strong familial support is necessary before the loved ones drifts into a world of their own. I have witnessed families coping with loved one who were diagnosed with Alzheimer. This disease does not discriminate.

I recall when I was head nurse in a neurological-behavioral unit. There were patients who were diagnosed with Alzheimer disease.

My primary responsibility was to ensure they received the highest standard of care. I remember these patients as if it were yesterday. This one patient was a senior civil engineer who was well respected because he designed one of the main freeways in this large city. His cognitive skills began to decline over the course of his employment with a large architectural firm. During weekly board meetings, his colleagues noticed he would forget his presentation. There were other patients who held professional jobs. There was a physician, an actor, and even a lawyer all were diagnosed with Alzheimer disease. One thing these families had in common; they all lack knowledge of the disease and the stages of the disease.

Once a loved one is diagnosed with Alzheimer, seek resources such as, local Alzheimer Associations, church ministries, and develop a weekly meeting with family members. This is important for the caregiver to involve as many family, friends, and church members as possible because support is needed from various sources to assist spiritually, emotionally, and physically. Decisions will have to be made. For instance, when is it appropriate to place the loved one in the hospital and even a nursing care facility. These decisions may become necessary especially for the caregiver when there is no family support. The caregiver will need assistance physically and emotionally. Understandably, feeling guilty is not uncommon when decisions have to be made. Reflect on those earlier years where you enjoyed each other. Reflecting on those earlier years is vital because you will be able to make those tough decisions when the time comes. Also, it is important to adhere to the loved one's wishes whether or not life support should be used when his/her condition becomes terminal.

Remember the biblical scripture. The Creator promises never to leave us. By reflecting on this scripture daily and daily prayer, you will make it through this season. Finally, when the time comes to say goodbye, give your loved one permission to leave.

# *Faith*

# Unfaithful Spouse/Divorced

We do not enter into marriage lightly. Once we enter in the union of holy matrimony, it is until death do us part; however, sometimes our marriage may end in a divorce. But it does not always have to end in a divorce provided the two parties are willing to work hard to save the marriage through prayers, and the advice of a marriage counselor. But most importantly, the couple should seek Christian counseling. Also, it is important to read the bible to ascertain what the scripture has to say about this institution called marriage.

**I Corinthians chapter 7 10**: *And unto the married, I command, yet, not I, but the Lord, let not the wife depart from her husband,* verse 12, *If any brother hath a wife that believeth not, and she be pleased to dwell with him, let him not put her away,* verse 13, *and the woman which hath an husband that believeth not, and if he be pleased to dwell with her, let her not leave him.*

**Adultery:** The bible speaks boldly about adultery in the marriage. It permits a spouse to be released of the mate for sexual immorality. This can be further explored in **Matthew 5:32 32** *"but I tell you that whoever puts away his wife, except for the cause of sexual immorality, makes* her an adulterous; and whoever marries her when she is put away commits adultery."

But even after one of the spouses have committed adultery, a marriage can still be saved through prayers, a forgiving spirit, a committed couple, a forgiving spouse, and continual Godly counseling. However, if one of the spouses is adamant in his/her decision to dissolve the marriage, accept the decision and allow in him/her to leave.

**Physical Abuse**: Being subjected to physical abuse is never acceptable or negotiable regardless of any circumstances because physical abuse can lead to death. The abused individual should seek safety immediately even if it means removing oneself in the presence of the abuser. This is not always possible if the abused spouse lacks economic support or immediate familial support. In this case, the church may be able to refer the abused spouse to organizations that may provide immediate shelter, employment etc.

The bible speaks concerning how marriage should be. In Ephesians **Chapter** 5 teaches that the husband is to cherish his wife. This means she is to be treated with tenderness and affection.

Remember love does not hurt but instead works relentlessly to give to please the other person.

Love never disserts, betray, or use another for selfish gain.

Love cherishes, love is proud and longed to be announced on top of Mount Everest.

Love is gentle, Love is kind, Love is patient, Love understands the other individual, Love honors, Love respects, Love is caring, and loves last until the end of the age.

## <u>NOTES:</u>

# NOTES:

# Faith

# Foreclosure Notice/ Eviction Notice

We work a lifetime hoping to enjoy the American dream of homeownership; however, because of the state of today's economy, employers are forced to lay off a substantial number of employees or cease operating and file for bankruptcy. We may find ourselves among the number of those who are unemployed. To compound the situation, employers are not hiring at the rate of the growing number of unemployment. When there is no longer a paycheck to pay the monthly mortgage, the financial institution forecloses on the mortgage loan. This is a major storm. Thoughts such as, *"where do I go? How embarrassing it will be having my neighbors seeing the foreclosure notice advertised in the paper*, but remember, He promises never to leave you and to be with you even to the end of the world.

Perhaps you exercised all of your options such as, home modification programs, borrowing from relatives, and you sought legal counseling. Because you no longer have sufficient income, you cannot afford further legal representation. This may be the time to release and let go. As strange as this may sound, this may be a blessing because it is when we are at our lowest ebb, it is then we depend wholeheartedly on the Lord. Now we can spend more time with Him verses having to work long hours on one job or having to work a second job just to maintain an image.

Where do you go from here? Seek listings for a low rental property. Or seek to relocate with family or close friends until you get back on your feet. But most importantly, you must exercise your faith more than ever. Believe this is a time of your life when you are beginning a new chapter in your life and the Creator will be with you regardless how hard it appears. The scripture in I Corinthian 5:7 tell us: *"We walk by faith not by sight."* Finally, remember:

**Roman 8: 28** tell us: *"And we know that in all things God works for the good of those who love him, who have been called according to His purpose."*

# NOTES:

# Faith

# Family Feuding

The family is the basic foundation of society. It is no wonder Satan attempts to break up families through divorce, separation, children being estranged from parents, misunderstanding of legal wills, and the list goes on and on that can result in family feuding.

What do we do? Regardless of the size of the family, there must be one individual who must attempt to keep the family intact. Some of the things that can cause family feud could stem from earlier years. For instance, may be one sibling believed the parent favored the other sibling and oppressed emotions that may have been transferred into adulthood. As a result, any incident that serves as a reminder of those early childhood may trigger an outburst. Perhaps the parent charged one of the siblings to be the executor of the family estate that may caused a family member to contest the Will. Maybe a family member did not feel a sense of belonging that was merely a misperception during those formidable years. There could be many reasons that could cause family feud, but one thing for sure—family feuding serves no positive rewards and must be dwelt with as quickly as possible.

What should be done during the first sign of feuding? Request a meeting to explore the root cause of the issue at-hand. One of the main reasons a family feud occurs is due to lack or breakdown in communication. Other tip that may prove helpful is to host monthly or quarterly family gatherings where each family member brings a covered dish. Also, it may be an excellent opportunity to begin a bible study. Pray for the family to come together because remember Satan loves to keep family apart—this is not the will of the Lord.

# NOTES:

# Faith

# Teenage Daughter becomes Pregnant

Marrying is sacred and having children and rearing them with love, guidance, and modeling a positive Christian-like behavior and values are most important. Sometimes the marriage dissolves leaving a single parent in the household to raise the children.

Divorce impacts the family spiritually, emotionally, and financially. The children may feel guilty and responsible for the divorce. Some children are affected to the point they feel unloved by the departing parent. The remaining parent maybe compelled to seek a second job to maintain the lifestyle or maintain basic living accommodations for the family. So the focus is shifted from family conferences to trying to make-ends meet. This sometimes results in children of divorced parents to seek love and acceptance from outside the family, peers. Let's face it; peer pressure is powerful especially when there is a breakdown in the family unit.

Teenage pregnancy, however, may occur when there are strong family ties even when both parents model Christian values; Sometimes parents are not comfortable talking about dating and abstaining from sexual intercourse until marriage with their children because of their upbringing. But as stated earlier, peer pressure can sometimes be more influential than parental guidance and not to mention today's culture where celebrities are choosing to forego marrying to become single parents.

I spoke with a few teenagers who were pregnant in their last trimester. I asked them was their pregnancies an accident or was it deliberate. I was amazed when half of those I interviewed informed me they wanted to become pregnant in order to have a child of their own, someone to love. I found their statements interesting.

How do you handle if your teenaged child becomes pregnant? Let your child know that you love her and you will support her. This is a very difficult time for her and she will need your love, prayer, and support for a long time. Help her to seek resources such as, parenting classes, comprehensive plan to return to school and if possible, make plans to involve the father and his parents. Teach your child to be a Godly parent. Encourage her to pray daily for a healthy child and for the Lord to keep her unborn child under His protection. Your faith will sustain you, your child, and your unborn grandchild.

# NOTES:

# Faith

# Child Gets Arrested

You raised your children the best you knew how based on the manner of you were raised. You model Christian values, but it appears regardless of your teachings, peer pressure was more powerful. Statistics reveal a child living in a home with a single parent is more at risk of dropping out of school and being arrested for committing a crime. Yet, I have met children who lived in a household with both parents, and yet they dropped out of school and some were arrested for minor and some major offenses. I was acquainted with other women who were head of household and their children never had any infractions and later went on to graduate from college. What do these different scenarios suggest?

Perhaps it means no one is exempt from children misbehaving. Remember we have an advocate who promises to remain with us until the end of the age. Let your child know you love them although you do not support his/her aberrant behavior that resulted in the arrest. Seek spiritual and professional counseling for your child to find the reason for your child's behavior. Try to get the child involve in a ministry at church, and most importantly, take time each day to sit down to talk to your child allowing him/her to talk openly and remember to listen. Finally, at the end of the day, kneel down and pray together. And before the child start his/her day, pray with them and ask the Lord to put a hedge of protection around them. You will see a positive change because the enemy cannot stand the power of prayer nor a united family.

Children are a gift from the Creator and we should rejoice because He entrusted us to guide and to lead them in the right manner. Remember in Matthews 18:3 when Jesus was asked by the disciples who would be the greatest in the kingdom when Jesus answered: "*I tell you the truth, unless you change and become like little children, you will never enter the kingdom of heaven. Therefore, whoever humbles himself like this child is the greatest in the kingdom of heaven.*"

# NOTES:

# Faith

# Family/Friend Betrays You

We create people the way we perceive them. Once our perception of the other person has been formed, we unconsciously program this imaginary being into our brains forever. Now the program is sealed and remains encapsulated within us. The program is stringent full of expectations of the other person. Unfortunately, it does not allow room for errors or deficiencies, and the individual is unaware of the expectations. Keep in mind; the program is based on our needs at the time the relationship was created. What is wrong with this picture? The other individual failed from the beginning; moreover, it is unfair to have unrealistic expectations to impose on another person. Additionally, the program failed to take into account the other individual is human with many frailties. What has transpired is that we create a perfect imaginary being who never existed.

Once the individual fails to live up to our expectations, we feel we have been betrayed. This could possibly be the reason why there are a high percentage of divorced couples, or perhaps the reason for break-ups of relationships both personally and professionally.

How to avoid creating an imaginary being?

Take the time to get to know the other person by having opened and frequent dialogue. Ask opened-ended questions about specific issues. For instance, you may ask:

1. "If you could find a way to cheat on your tax returns and no one would ever know would you do it?"
2. Do reflective listening. For example, he may respond to the question: "That depends" . . . You may respond by asking: 'Depends?" "Would you explain?"
3. Watch the person's behavior towards the way he/she treats others. For example, do you observe rude behavior? Is the individual rude to those he/she comes in to contact with in the market? or while driving when someone attempts to change lanes in front of them? Does this person do acts of kindness to the needy?
4. Observe the individual's relationship with his/her parents. If male, does he have a close and loving relationship with his mother? If female, does she have this same type of relationship with her father? Parental relationship is vital because the manner of which the individual treats the parents will be replicated in the two of your relationship.
5. Inquire about the character of the individuals' father or mother. For example, does the father cheats on his mother, or does the individual's mother cheats on the father. This information may be helpful to determine if patterns have been established as the norm in the individual's household that could possibly be carried over into his/her lifestyle with you.

6. Observe how the individual pays his/her bills. Are they responsible? Do they have a good credit score? Also, observe whether they give to charity organizations.

7. If you are engaged and the other individual was married previously, you may want to talk to the divorced spouse to get ideas to learn the reason they divorced.

8. Listen to determine what is the bulk of their conversation—count the number of times the pronoun" I' is used in the course of a conversation.

9. Finally, if you are planning to marry the person, seek Christian counseling, and pray and fast and ask the Lord to grant you a discerning spirit of whether or not this person is the right mate.

## <u>NOTES:</u>

## NOTES:

# Faith

# Deciding to Resign/Relocate

Deciding to resign from your current job to relocate can be intimidating. After all, you are familiar with this job and all of the intricate details, and the city has become your home for more than five years. Yet you were offered a substantial pay increase.

What should you do?

The first thing to do is to pray and seek the Will of the Lord. Second, make a list of pros and cons to determine which one outweighs the other. Ask yourself if money is the impetus that is causing you to consider this change. Should money be the sole driving force for you to change jobs and relocate? It is prudent to compare the cost of living between the two cities. Also, analyzed the city you are considering relocating to and determine the average price of a home, the cost of food, automobile insurance, and the price of gasoline per gallon.

Remaining on one job for over five years may or may not be beneficial depending on the company's goal, mission, and retirement plan.

Also, it is vital to determine if there is opportunity for upward mobility, and if there is reorganization underway that could possibly means your job could be outsourced. Are you growing by learning new skill-sets that will make you marketable in the workforce? Once you have done your research, prayed, and analyzed these questions, you should reach an intelligent and spiritual decision. Regardless of the decision you make, we stand on His promises that He is Omnipotent (all power), Omniscient (all knowing), and Omnipresent (everywhere).

## NOTES:

# Faith

# Having to Suddenly Live Alone

Living alone is a process that requires adjusting especially if you are suddenly faced with living alone due to a death, divorce, or the result of being a victim of an empty nest. In order to overcome the loneliness and emptiness, pray to the Creator and tell him you are frightened and depending on Him. This is a vulnerable period because an individual could easily slip into depression.

How do you live alone?

1. Think of your safety; ensure you have a workable alarm system. Change your answering service voicemail to record the voice of a standard greeting during your absence or when you are on the phone.
2. During home repairs, never let the technician know that you live alone. You may ask a neighbor's husband or male relative to come over during repairs.
3. Leave a light on front and rear of your home at dust.

4. Get involved in a social group at a local chapter such as, volunteering at the local Red Cross, church organization, or volunteering in school. This new affiliation will assist you to establish new friends and keep you occupied. At the end of the day, you will fall asleep with ease.

5. Cook. Some individuals who live alone stop cooking, but you should continue cooking for the simply reason you need the proper nutrition, and it will prevent you from eating fast food that will contribute to those unwanted pounds and elevate your cholesterol level. Also, the smell of food cooking in a home lifts depression. It has been reported when a house is on the market for sell, when potential buyers are greeted with the aroma of food, they are more likely to purchase the home.

6. Finally at the end of the day, read a scripture each night and pray for the Lord to protect you while you sleep. Afterwards, leave the bible opened not only in your bedroom but throughout your house. Remember when you are feeling lonely and fearful, the bible tells us:

"The angel of the Lord encamps around those who fear him, and He delivers them."

**Psalms 34:7:**

# NOTES:

# Faith

# Singleness

Living single is a gift as mentioned in the bible, 1 Corinthians 7; 7-8. No two persons are alike; one person may not have any problem living alone, going to movies, eating alone in a restaurant, or taking a cruise alone, yet another individual would whether sit at home alone before considering going to any venue without an escort.

Women are outnumbering men during weekly church service, and it appears more women than men are enrolling in institution of higher learning; moreover, it is reported there is a high percentage of African American males dropping out of high schools. So females are finding themselves going solo when attending special events, and find themselves surrounded by more females than males when attending colleges and universities.

Men may also find it challenging meeting women in spite of the ratio of women to men. Some men may be taciturn, insecure when it comes to meeting women, uncertain on how to approach the opposite sex, or fear of being rejected. Perhaps that may be the reason there are growing number of men joining dating sites, and social networks in an attempt to meeting a compatible mate. Yet I often ask why would a man resort to such dating and social networks hoping to meet females when there is a large population of single women? Perhaps single women should ask themselves the same question before accessing such social networks.

If you are single, don't give-up. Do not allow meeting a mate consume you to the point you are failing to miss the beauty that surrounds you such as, family, friends, co-workers, and an opportunity to leave a legacy by making a difference in someone's life who are less fortunate than you. Remember we are all placed on this earth for a purpose. Until you have fulfilled your purpose which the Lord has for your life, you may never find that soul mate. For instance, let say you graduated from college and you decided to teach because teaching is your passion. Have you thought about volunteering to teach at a local Urban League for trouble teens? What about using your skill-sets to teach a Sunday School Class? When you began to remove yourself from the equation and to concentrate on helping others, you are not only fulfilling your destiny, but you radiate a natural beauty that attracts others especially the opposite sex. There is a saying. "I was not looking and yet love found me."

Heather Mills is a leading charity and animal rights campaigner. She works internationally, raising funds to establish global locations to help amputees obtain new limbs. One day as she was speaking to a group, Paul McCartney was impressed with her and after researching, obtained her phone number and later phoned her and asked her out on a date. She thought it was a prank call until he finally convinced her he was Paul McCartney. The two married. Unfortunately the marriage would dissolve, but the fact she met a mate when she was providing a service to others and in spite of the divorce, she was put on the radar where she is attracting men who desire to date her. So if you find yourself single, concentrate on first building the kingdom by seeking ways to helping others verses spending a lifetime concentrating on being single and meeting someone.

## NOTES:

## NOTES:

# Faith

# Chaos in the Workplace

The workplace is not always pleasant. In view of the state of the economy, employees may feel frightened of losing their jobs because of the daily demands to increase productivity. Such demands can make the work environment chaotic and stressful; moreover, it may cause employees to compete with one another to the point employees may be driven to put one another down just to make them standout. This type of behavior serves no purpose, and in the long run, fails to foster a team approach and decreases overall morale and productivity. These types of employees fail to realize this is not the way to succeed. Proverbs 1:19 identify them: *So are the ways of everyone who is greedy for gain; it takes away the life of its owners."*

In addition to working in a competitive work environment among co-workers, you may have a supervisor who lacks leadership skills who shows favoritisms to a select group of employees. The supervisor may develop personal relationships with some employees and a dislike for others. Another example is when the supervisor fails to apply standards consistently to every employee when contributing work assignment.

Also, during time to evaluate employees, the supervisor may rely on hear say information from other employees to assist in evaluating employees. Finally, when the company is faced with reduction in force due to declining revenue and collections, supervisors may be asked to reduce the percentage of workforce. Who is most likely to be given the ax? Those employees who are less favored.

What do you do if you find yourself in a situation where you are not part of a select group of employees in the workplace?

Never compromise the basic rule to treat others the way you desire to be treated. Let's face it; you may not be favored for no particular reason. You may be disliked because of the way you articulate, dress, the manner in which you conduct yourself, the fact you are a believer and do not compromise your values, or perhaps you may be more knowledgeable of what the job entails than co-workers and supervisor, or you may resemble an individual the supervisor encountered in the past where the relationship was negative. Regardless of the supervisor's behavior, you should perform the job to the best of your ability because you are not working for man but you represent a much higher calling. This attitude will help you to excel in any career path you choose to take. I understand first-hand how un-pleasant it is to work in an environment when the supervisor lacks basic leadership skills. I worked for many organizations and I experienced inconsistency and unfair treatment in the workplace. This is the way I coped during those tumultuous years.

Each morning prior to going to work, I prayed and asked the Lord to give me the will and wisdom to do my job effectively in His honor and to let everything I touch prosper regardless of the complexity of the assignment. I asked Him to help me to respond in love to those I was in daily contact with including the supervisor and co-workers. Once I arrived on the job, I would tear a small piece of paper and write these five words: "The Lord is my shepherd." Afterwards, I placed the piece of paper in my pocket. I wanted those words close to me to help guide me in every situation I may encounter that day. Over the years, I found countless pieces of paper in my clothing that reminded me how He protected me during those challenging years. Once I arrived on the job, I prayed silently as I performed my work each day. On one particular job, I recall I was least favored in spite of my performance of making this company large amount of money. I was transferred to a department of which I had no experience. Eventually I would go on to resign and went on to do exceptionally well in my career because I did the best I could on that job. Shortly after my departure, the company recognized how valuable I had been, and they felt the financial impact. Why? Because I was a winner, a child of the most high, I could never lose. I am reminded of the scripture: *He is a shield to those who work uprightly.* Proverbs 2:7. I received countless phone calls from a plethora of companies inviting me to work for them.

Sometimes you may feel like you are being crucified in the workplace, but remember "No cross no crown." You will always be successful if you continue to follow biblical principles and apply them in every aspects of your life. Sometimes, the best thing an employer can do is to set you free from an unequally yoke work environment. If you find yourself unemployed, refer to those steps given earlier in this book. Never give up because He will be with you until the end of the age.

# NOTES:

# NOTES:

# Faith

# Funds Depleted/
# Early Retirement

You planned to retire at an old rightful age, but instead, you took early retirement because of the demands that were forced on you-if you remained on the job, you may have been terminated with loss of benefits. Now you receive monthly retirement benefits, but it is hardly enough to pay your monthly expenses; moreover, you are too young for Social Security Benefits. What do you do when funds are being depleted and monthly expenses continue?

First pray to the almighty to let Him know you are helpless and have nowhere to go but to Him.

Update your resume focusing on your skill—sets that will make you marketable such as, computer skills, Excel, Microsoft etc.

Contact three individuals you are confident will give you a good reference, but first ask them.

Look for service-based employments. For example, apply for the night shift as a clerk in the emergency room of a local hospital or nursing home, or fast food chain.

Complete your tax return early especially if you due a refund. This would be a great opportunity for you to request an application to work as a seasonal worker as a local tax preparer.

This may seem strange, but plan to give ten per cent of your monthly income to the church or to charity. It is God promise to us if we give 10% of the first fruit, He would open up a window of bountiful blessings that we would not have room to receive them. Do this lovingly not grudgingly.

I recall years early when my employer announced there would be a substantial number of layoffs due to the decline in revenue collections. I begin to imagine my being unemployed with a desire to give to the church but couldn't. So, I started to give 10% of my income to the church. I was not laid off that year. It was seven years later when my employer outsourced my department and moved me to another department of which I was unfamiliar with the activities and not to mention the volume of work. But remember the number seven is the year of completion. Consequently, I was prepared to retire that year and my savings and monthly benefits were adequate to satisfy my monthly expenses. The Lord remembered how faithful I had been, and He was not going to forsake me. He will remember you too provided you remain faithful.

"I will never leave you nor forsake you"

**Hebrew 13:5, 6**

## NOTES:

# Faith

# Forgiveness

It is not always easy to forgive or to forget when we have been hurt by someone. Sometimes we spend a lifetime holding a grudge. This is not healthy nor is it productive. When we hold hate or resentment towards another, we internalize this emotion and cause ourselves to succumb slowly because we cannot enjoy life to the fullest. It affects an individual physically to the point he/she becomes ill. For example, an individual may have migraine headaches, ulcers, hypertension, depression, and many other disorders. When a person is ill, he/she is unable to perform at his/her optimal level. This means the person who hurt you has taken complete control over your future because you failed to forgive; instead, you chose to carry this burden for years. Sadly, the person who hurt you may be unaware he/she hurt you, or may be the individual is no longer alive.

How do you forgive?

First, you must recognize in order to live a healthy life and to live according to the purpose the Creator designed for your life, you must be willing to forgive. Second, you must accept the fact the individual who hurt you may be unaware of his/her action or the individual may not be capable of discerning his/ her action was hurtful. Pray that individual will change his/her behavior and enter into a relationship with the Lord. Then pray for you to forgive that person.

Our lives are destined with a purpose by the Creator for our very existence. It would be futile if we come to the end of life never knowing the purpose of our lives because we spent a lifetime refusing to forgive.

One chaplain wrote an article describing how he witnessed countless deaths during the course of his lifetime. He explained individuals who were at peace with family and friends had a more peaceful death opposed to individuals who had not made peace. He explained individuals who failed to forgive or desired forgiveness often struggled and fought to live during that final hour.

—

# NOTES:

# Faith

# Alcoholism

Alcohol is a drug and once consumed it is absorbed in the body with affect on major organs. We all have the choice to choose whether or not to drink alcohol. It is unknown why some individuals who drink never become an alcoholic and others who drink eventually become an alcoholic.

Alcoholism is a debilitative disease when an individual has an addiction to alcohol. This disease should be among the nomenclature of the classification of diseases such as, heart attack, sickle cells anemia, and many other conditions.
Deciding to drink should be weighed seriously because studies suggest there is a genetic disposition that suggests if one parent is an alcoholic the greater the risk for a child becoming an alcoholic.

Drinking excessively over a prolong period of time can prove to be harmful to the body. I have witnessed so many patients in the hospital who suffered cirrhosis of the liver a (hardening of the liver), and other complications such as gastrointestinal disorders. The greatest risk is cirrhosis. It is amazing how the liver can withstand chronic abuse over a period of years, but when an individual becomes a chronic excessive drinker, the liver cannot sustain its normal function.

How do you help an individual who is an alcoholic? The first thing is to recognize alcoholism is a disease. Oftentimes the individual may not recognize he/she is an alcoholic. Individuals may think they can stop drinking anytime they choose, but this is the farthest from the truth. Help the individual to identify their drinking pattern and encourage and provide them literature to read about alcohol and the risk of alcoholism. Be supportive of the individual but do not be an enabler. Pray with the individual to desire to stop drinking especially if they show early signs of alcoholism. Once you have provided support and resources, pray for the individual to see the need to curtail drinking. Remember it is up to the individual to desire to live in sobriety.

# NOTES:

# Faith

# Summary

Storms of life are inevitable for each of us, but we have an advocate who promises to be with us even to the end. He died for us on Calvary's cross because He loved us. He paid the ultimate price with the shedding of His blood, and by His blood, we are made whole. The storms will come but regardless of the number of times we find ourselves facing them, we know that we are more than conqueror because we are the seed of Abraham, so that makes us part of the Royal Family. What the enemy meant for bad, we know the Lord will turn it around for our good. The enemy comes to us in different forms as this book outlined. The enemy is sickness, loss of employment, loneliness, death of a love one, and depletion of funds. But if we keep our focus on the Savior, we will defeat any obstacle that the enemy places before us. We are, however, obligated to serve the master even in the middle of our stormy season by serving one another. When we serve, we are fulfilled; we have a sense of peace and our storms seem to vanish because we redirect our focus from ourselves to others. We are obligated to serve the least of these because **Matthews Chapter 25: 40** reminds us: 'Truly I tell you, whatever you did for one of the least of these brothers and sisters of mine, you have done it unto me." With an unwavering faith and belief that our Lord and Savior died on the cross and were raised and that He Promises to never to leave us, you will have peace and be victorious. Now you are equipped to go through any storm with confidence knowing you have an advocate who promises to never forsake you. Now you can faith it all!

Source:
Holy Bible New King James Version